1972

This book may be

PHILOSOPHY

FOR THE NEW AGE

PHILOSOPHY
FOR
THE NEW AGE

ALAN FLETCHER MARKUN

PHILOSOPHICAL LIBRARY
New York

CONTENTS

PREFACE

In the month of September 1963, "The New Revolution" was published by Philosophical Library. Since that time many changes have occurred throughout our country and the world, some of them foretold and brought about by this book.

Though acclaimed by many, certain facts regarding The New Revolution were never generally known. Occasionally in history there are works that have required guides or a sequel. Milton's "Paradise Lost" and "Paradise Regained" in literature; Newton's physical laws and mathematics in science; programme visualis in operatic and classical music, and works in philosophy such as those of Kant and Spinoza.

My reasons for elucidating upon these matters now are threefold: First, enough years have elapsed since publication of The New Revolution, that it can now be told. Secondly I have been urged by so many of my readers to continue writing (I had already dismantled most of my reference library)—and thirdly, and probably most important, I feel that I owe it to the world, so that future generations may better understand and evaluate the philosophy of The New Revolution.

FOREWORD

The original purposes in creating "The New Revolution" were to probe for truth, educate fellow human beings, and place in the world a catalyst for change. The latter could not be mentioned at the time, as such.

Philosophy, as we understand the word to mean today, is usually a search for meaning to life, for truth. It is not limited as to method—and the number of possible methods are many. Truth itself, being in this life largely relative, has a number of possible degrees.

PHILOSOPHY

FOR THE NEW AGE

SECTION I

Many scholars of renown have stated through the years, that in a lifetime, few human beings, even intellectuals, employ over a small fraction of their full mental capacities. In my younger days I often wondered about this, what might be done were an individual to employ his full mental powers. I had just an average mind, and a little higher education (which was interrupted by World War II). I was not, though, satisfied with the world about me, or with the extent of my own understanding. After long and searching thought, and a difficult decision I embarked upon an experiment. Herein lie the unique properties of "The New Revolution."

I set forth upon an endeavor to better understand life, which in turn entailed much study and thought. This led into a number of fields, philosophy being one of them. Over the years, through a variety of means, I managed to gradually activate my full mental resources, and employ them in this endeavor and subsequently in the production of The New Revolution. It was a long but fruitful search—which took me into strange places, broad vistas, and obscure byways of thought. The undertaking was similar in some respects to a military campaign—wherein I launched an assault against the barriers of life that conceal its mysteries. In it was the thrust, later consolidation, retrenchment, etc.

It required a combination of methods to reach, activate, and employ the deep mental powers that in most people remain dormant. Will-power, sublimation, a sense of purpose, and that exquisite ecstasy and pain so common to creative artists, revolutionaries and religious zealots—these were but a few of the methods, albeit the major ones. By sublimating (turning inward) the sexual urge, I was able over part of the time to make available for my work vast amounts of raw energy! This is a perilous course, but I did it and it can be done.

Throughout history a small percentage of human beings have used their full mental capabilities. Socrates, Plato, Euclid, Hegel, Hume, Newton, Dickens, Shakespeare, Nietzsche, Einstein—to mention but a few, these men possessed genius. Some used their full abilities, others did not. In my case I did not possess genius, but by marshalling my full mental capacity over a protracted period of time I was able to reach a high plateau, maybe even approach the genius level, and remain there temporarily.

A vast amount of thought, study and research were required—lasting eighteen years, to completion of the book, and representing the sum total of my life experiences to that date. There is corroborating testimony regarding this, including public records. The adventure was debilitating to me physically, and very hard generally, but the task was finally accomplished—and without benefit from hallucinatory drugs, alcohol, or narcotics, which I have never used. It was a deep probe into the nature of things by a mind pushed to its utmost limit.

The New Revolution was able finally to look beyond the paradoxes of this life, into realms of the unknown—to discern some of its realities. This is why some of the conclusions may seem strange, even naive at times—because they actually reach past the truths and paradoxes that we know and are familiar with. The importance of these factors can hardly be overstated. Several of the conclusions I do not understand myself. Perhaps someday a "Rosetta Stone" will be found that will unlock some of these mysteries.

There is a central theme running through The New Revolution, just as in a concerto—though it was broken in places to permit byroads and digression into wider areas of thought. One might note that at times The New Revolution may have seemed disconnected or rather carelessly put together. I think this myself. Thus, I cannot fully defend some of these factors, other than to say that—my mind extended to its farthest limit, dictated the ways these things should be.

Examples of pertinence might be the way a sudden solution comes to a struggling scientist; or an inspiration come to an aspiring poet. Still another example might be the manner in which communications come to a spiritualist medium—and if honesty prevails, the medium will relay these messages verbatum. The communications are often garbled, and frequently out of their correct time order. Yet, more likely than not, the messages do come from somewhere beyond and manifest a degree of truth.

For my part, I made every effort in The New Revolution to sort out and keep ideas in their correct time sequence. Even so however, some of them extended past our time and place. The New Revolution actually illuminated more through a series of sudden flashes, rather than as one continuous light. And while many of my positions were reasoned out painstakingly, inch at a time—some were attained with a leap and bound. In finality, The New Revolution was primarily a creative work, rather than a critical study, though it was tempered by history and fact. There is an area, however, wherein I think the work to be deficient (several others have voiced this opinion)—and that is in its period content (historical detail). This may be. Of course, content varies from book to book, as does fact and presentation. It depends too upon what one is looking for.

There is good and bad in The New Revolution, just as there is good and bad in life. It seemed to me that philosophy should parallel or at least reflect life, and throughout life there is both good and evil (as we know them). And since mine was a total commitment—then there was inevitably both good and bad present, serenity and violence, sense and nonsense, logic and emotionalism. And to remain consistent with life it was necessary that these paradoxes appear not in just one area of The New Revolution, but be interwoven throughout. This is extraordinary for a literary work, and very likely the only philosophy of its kind in the world. It was thus a sort of imitation of life.

Emerson stated that "Evermore in the world is this marvellous balance of beauty and disgust, magnificence and rats." This is a good description and composite picture of life on this earth. In war we wound and slay our enemies, and they do the same to us, each considering the other to be bad. In hygiene we wash and scrub our skins until sometimes they become almost sterile, yet deep inside our bodies—germs, viruses and bacteria thrive and putrefaction takes place. Good and bad are of course relative terms, depending for their meaning upon varying sets of circumstances. In short, good and bad (as we know them) are inextricably bound together in this life, and to live we must accept both. Of course we try to minimize the bad.

Most philosophies throughout history have been of a theoretical orientation, and often very limited—some concerning little more than form and substance. Regarding philosophies in general, the types are varied. For example, political philosophies, while usually close to the people, are at the same time too crude and limited to qualify as philosophies of life; social philosophies are too terrestrial, and religious philosophies too inflexible and narrow. In many philosophies a prescribed system is set forth, such as:

Platonism, Romanticism, Mysticism, Pragmatism, etc., and a definite method established such as induction or deduction.

In The New Revolution there was no prescribed system or any one exclusive method, because it is a philosophy of individualism and diversity. There were some parts overly abstract for the average person, however most of the work dealt with everyday life. The New Revolution was never meant as a manual to lead the way—but rather as a light to illuminate, so that each individual as well as the masses of people can better find their way.

Many times people's decisions regarding problems and judgment of the future are influenced incorrectly by current conditions that prevail yet are temporary, and not necessarily typical of other areas. This affects every field of human endeavor, and is precisely where history comes in as an invaluable aid. The New Revolution is eclectic, employing bits of truth wherever they were found. In politics, commerce, war—opportunities are seized as they present themselves. This same phenomenon is seen in science, and can be utilized in philosophy. Truth is where we find it, whether it be in a lecture hall or a city hall, an airport or a sea town. We should probe as many fields as possible and utilize method too—however when we come upon truth we should never turn our backs because of the manner in which it is attired.

In outlooks, philosophies, and famous strategies of history, particularly those dealing with limited objectives such as political campaigns or winning a war—while often vitally important, these still can never afford the luxury of diversity possible for a philosophy of life. A philosophy of life should, I think, cover the widest possible range—even if some subjects must be treated superficially. Because life is made up of so many things; and although the gulf separating the varying viewpoints may be wide, sometimes common denominators can be found.

One critic stated of The New Revolution that it went too deep, thereby getting out of touch with everyday realities. Another critic said that The New Revolution dealt too much with everyday problems (he favored abstraction). Still another stated that while there is much truth throughout The New Revolution, it should best be read by expert and analytical readers. It is true, in intellectual work there are always these possibilities. However there was much to be gained by going deep and reaching far—and that was in getting to the roots of things, the causes of events on this earth. As a result, it becomes possible to better understand life, and to a lesser or greater extent, correct some of its problems.

The third and last major factor regarding The New Revolution that must be explained is the activistic aspect or catalytic effect. I felt that since the notorious evils of this world are so large and so deeply entrenched—and since so many great people throughout history have made so many attempts to change this, usually in vain—then a direct or regular assault by myself would be futile. But by taking a different, seldom used route, and attacking from an unusual angle, perhaps some good could be achieved. Granted, I could not bring in conventional fire power this way, over these small back roads—but by having the elements of surprise on my side, and appearing from an unexpected quarter, some success was accomplished. First, I felt that shock should be used to shake and storm their bastions. The more fearsome one can appear in such an undertaking, the better. Second, I felt that to be effective one would have to concentrate upon important and strategic areas, and that could best be done by the use of catalytic agents. Catalytic agents are usually small entities that can set off large effects, e.g. the enzyme.

These pertinent facts could not be told before, because they would have reduced the effectiveness of the writing as a catalytic agent for change. I would liken The New Revolution to a storm cloud, that contained many properties, some of which could not be identified at the time. Throughout The New Revolution the usual method employed for bringing about catalytic effects was distortion of emphasis. It should be pointed out that every system ever employed by man upon this earth, has been a distortion of historical patterns. My stratagem called for a delicate balance to be maintained through most of the book, in order to attain catalytic effects and yet remain consistent with fact. The work, while completely candid in most areas, is weighted in others, overplayed at times, underplayed at other times, carefully stationed—so as to cause shock, anger, ferment, challenge, and thereby change. Several of the major means employed toward this end were terror, threat, and challenge. As is well known, the various powers in human society become entrenched, and surround themselves with thick fortress walls. If ever they are to be routed or even shaken, a heavy blow must be struck.

For example where I detailed scenes of carnage and war, it was to cause shock and disgust. And in a sense of challenge, I am reminded of a case I once knew, of a drunkard who was saved from that awful fate by a friend. One day the friend shamed the drunkard in front of the latter's friends—calling him a hopeless, sickening mess, too weak and cowardly to pull himself together. The strategy, fortunately, worked as the friend had hoped—the drunkard became angry, finally asserted his will and in due time did improve and become a responsible citizen again.

When, in The New Revolution, I struck at religion and its vast hypocrisy, it was necessary, as religion had become a great roadblock, beyond which little of value could proceed. Over the centuries the society of man has built religious dogma into a huge idol, suffocating the real religious teachings beneath, irrational and tyrannical in general. It served one overriding purpose, that of perpetuating the evils of the world, while holding the real religion in thraldom. My attack was primarily in the nature of a challenge for religion to grow fearful of the masses it had betrayed, and disgusted by its own sad condition, thus to rise up and overthrow its oppressors—and become more honest, tolerant, benevolent, peaceloving.

The everyday, secular forces of the world have always exploited and used religion for their own selfish ends. They wanted the clergy to be ineffectual and preoccupied with unimportant things. They wanted the churches to give their blessings to whatever those in power did, and usually they received those blessings. This in turn embedded the evils so deeply in the social structure, that virtually nothing could change them. Organized religion is not blameless however, for they acquiesced too easily and offered little resistance. Compromises are one thing, a complete sellout quite another. So even a reduction in their power, which I urged—would be a first and necessary step toward reform.

Religion has had a terrible history, though it also has a great potential for good, if used properly. The New Revolution bore a spiritual message—but since the usual spiritual theme is not listened to today, I felt it necessary to phrase and word my message differently. Gandhi is reputed to have said that he likes our Jesus, but not our Christianity. He went on to say that Christianity is like a vaccination—that prevents the real Christian teaching from coming through and succeeding.

When I referred to the multitudes who hate religion, and spoke of the churches' demise, again I did so to cause shock and a catalytic effect—forcing religion to act, throw off its exploiters and choose reform. Remember, only as far back as 1963 one could not safely talk of such things—as have since that time occurred! Needless to say, the powerful religious bigots needed to be cut down to size—and they were. It could not, however, have been done with a mild or meek attack. Martin Luther's antagonism with the church was primarily over dogma and ritual. My argument has been with these, and with morals and ethics as well.

Two outstanding examples of distortion and resultant catalytic effects, which undoubtedly were sought, are— Stephen Crane's celebrated poem "If War Be Kind" and "Grass" the famous poem by Carl Sandburg. Regarding stimuli toward motivation, much is also a matter of interpretation. Phenomena are interpreted differently by different people. For example the statement by Patrick Henry ". . . Give me liberty or give me death" is regarded by most people as being one of the pillars of our freedom. But a reactionary person might interpret the statement as an admonition to rebel against restraints that the majority had long ago accepted as necessary and desirable.

When, in The New Revolution, I struck at women and their false morality—that too was a challenge to them to improve, to become freer, more peaceloving, tolerant and wise. When I attacked private organizations, it was because at that time the far right was building a dangerous network of subversive groups. The attack was crude, but I felt that it was justified.

When I spoke disparagingly of some elements of the Negro race—it was entirely in the nature of a challenge. Also, that was before Martin Luther King had begun attacking the war making system, an attack which I later applauded loudly.

And even retribution that I recommended for the future, to be directed against political and social reaction and militarism, was primarily as a stimulus toward reform, and only secondarily as a deterrent to discourage people from following those paths.

I might add that there is no exaggeration or, so far as I know, other underlying technique used throughout this thesis. These are my candid views on the subjects concerned, and I will not renege on them. This is both an affidavit and a chart to show the way.

SECTION II

This section corresponds with Chapter II of The New Revolution. Regarding the nature of life, I want to say, that in terms of logic, I incline toward thinking the Theory of Reincarnation to be essentially true. It is not only probably the most logical theory of life, but there is some very substantial evidence in its favor, a factor that most other theories lack. Reduced to relatively simple terms, the Theory of Reincarnation states that the individual soul is eternal and that it absorbs and retains the experiences of this and other lives, and gradually evolves from the low plane of this world to higher planes. There may also be merit in the Macrocosm-Microcosm Theory, and in the possibility of other dimensions. I believe that there is a Supreme Power and universal plan, but our mentalities are too limited to perceive it. I think, too, that fate plays an important part in our lives, and the Hindus call this Karma, the eternal chain of cause and effect.

Out of body experiences, such as many people have had, I think prove something. LSD has made some of these possible, and apparently all are not hallucination. I think that this tends to show that we are really something distinctly different from our bodies. And there are such things as ghosts. This phenomenon is most likely a manifestation of the second body or etheric double, that, according to occult teachings everyone possesses. This ethereal body is a vehicle for the next higher plane, and disintegrates eventually, just as the material body of this world does. In ghost manifestations the ethereal body somehow becomes visible to us or influences our senses in some other manner—and its recurrence may span long periods of time.

Many famous people throughout history, people whose word in other fields we bank upon every day, have believed in continued existence after bodily death—and not a few of them have had supernormal experiences. Numerous biographies substantiate this. Several of the founders of modern Psychology supported as fact, certain of the seance occurrences. I myself can vouch for ghost phenomena, because I once lived for several years in a house that was haunted—yes —really haunted. Another factor that I think worthy of mention are the various types of curses. There is much credible evidence in the world as to their efficacy, and doubters have sometimes paid dearly. A curse somehow puts into motion forces that we do not yet understand. This again falls within the field of Para-psychology.

Generally speaking I incline toward feeling that there is also some truth to Dunne's Serial Universe theory, and in my own Dream Hypothesis, although at what level of existence I cannot say. There must be a number of states of being, possibly inter-connected.

The materialistic philosophy states that when we die that is the end of us. I do not believe this, because there is considerable evidence to the contrary. Today science postulates the existence of a force they call "anti-matter" a mirror image of matter. Which raises queries as to whether such laws as The Second Law of Thermodynamics are universal—and whether the past and future are really as far separated as was once believed. Another theory is that we are the remnants of colonists or castaways from an advanced race dwelling far away in space—or that we are its vassals. Even were this true, we still might be subject to reincarnation, and so might they.

24

In pondering the imponderable, one is always wont to come into trouble, however this is the way it is. Any position regarding a hereafter, by contemporary standards, cannot be positively proved or disproved. In discussing possible attributes of the ultimate, one might, as many philosophers have done, enumerate various possibilities: indifference, powerless, experimenting, insane, evil, manifest by reincarnation, incomprehensible, many gods, no god. Of these I would have to choose experimenting, manifest by reincarnation, and incomprehensible.

About the total of history, little is known. There are ruins in many parts of the world, so ancient that no one can even guess as to their origin. Few people know the full history of their own countries, and few of us know the past history of our own communities. I recall a discussion once regarding the history of a small town of less than one hundred families. It soon became apparent that the complete history would be so voluminous as to be well beyond us. What does all this imply? I think that the only lasting history must be our individual memories.

From birth we are forced into a mold by the sheer weight of long standing custom, a tortuous pattern that imposes its particular shape upon us. Most creatures follow this pattern throughout life, and perhaps this is as it should be. A small number of humans, though, rebel, and perhaps this too is as it should be. It takes courage and stamina to rebel, and much more stamina yet to remain outside of the pattern. This is a fact of life, and certainly suggests that it is survival and wellbeing of the group that is primary in this world. Development of the self though is important too, because it may be the primary factor after this life. Those who think that their lives could not possibly have any lasting significance, may be wrong.

I might add by way of footnote, for those not too familiar

25

with the Theory of Reincarnation, that one does not have to be a Hindu in order to believe. The theory has a vast following the world over, including hundreds of thousands in our own country. Many of them belong to Theosophical groups, located in numerous cities. Some may be found in groups interested in Spiritualism.

SECTION III

As enigmatical as it may sound, I firmly believe that the emotions are truer than reasoning, at least so far as this life is concerned. Emotions are generally thought of as being basic, akin to instincts—whereas reasoning is usually cultivated. Some emotions though are also cultivated. Although there may be a certain logic to the functioning of this world, we cannot see it. The everyday life in our civilization is governed almost exclusively by emotions, illusions, ideologies, images, mystiques. Politics, war, the creative elements of society, style, the entertainment world—all of these are governed thus. Even as staid a world as the stock market is influenced—and in the area of jurisprudence, it is only too well known how emotions affect juries. Fine logic and mathematical exactitude are important, in fact imperative in modern civilization—yet so far as major decisions are concerned, they are still far in the background. In many matters logical reasoning carries the day, but in the most basic and important decisions made by individuals and even by groups, emotions usually dominate.

Sometimes the emotions err, but reasoning can also err. Often behavior of people is classed as emotional, when in reality it is response based upon harmful, irrational, or outdated education. For example, there was a time when the socially proper response to a slight affront, was the challenge to a duel. This was not usually emotional, but instead the product of false ideals. There was a time when the socially acceptable response to crises was for the female to faint. This was seldom emotional, but instead the result of conditioned response and false ideals. Later, even into today, the

27

socially acceptable response to shock on the part of the female is to scream. Again this is the result of false ideals—and, with the advance of women, is now rapidly disappearing. Of course, in all human behavior, the desired response would be an amalgamation of emotion and reason —and this is what we strive for.

As I stated in The New Revolution, survival of the fittest among human beings, is largely a matter of circumstances. For example, a three hundred pound muscular man would have been very fit to survive in pre-historic times or even in ancient times—but a one hundred and fifty pound skilled swordsman would have been far better fit for survival in the Middle Ages, and a skilled maker of armor, even better fit for survival. And a one hundred pound skilled technician in one of the sciences, either male or female, will be better fit for survival today.

Many have been the teachings that have influenced the civilization of man. Most of the celebrated among them have covered long periods of time, but have often confined themselves largely to particular geographical areas. Of all the individual philosophers though throughout history, the one who I think displayed extraordinary power was Nietzsche. This is why I discuss his work.

When Nietzsche fairly shouted "Man is something that shall be overcome"—what was this but a vision? In that day, to write such a thing, required more than the accumulated knowledge of higher learning had yet to offer. And what was Zarathustra but a mystic? Much of the lofty verbalisms and guidance that he espoused could easily be fit into scripture, except regarding the intangible. Zarathustra, man of the ages, sojourning among his people like an ancient prophet. And even his parables were cause for wonder. When he met the old saint in the wilderness and they discoursed as equals, does this not display some of Nietzsche's true thinking? Nietzsche himself, however, seemed to favor an ethic, but devoid of non-material implication.

And when Nietzsche through his prophet Zarathustra did shout "Behold, I teach you the overman: he is this lightning, he is this frenzy,"—this was perhaps the most powerful bit of literary rhetoric ever uttered. It should, as its background, have had the booming of the drums of Thor!—or did it? And what was Zarathustra but a profound thinker? Nietzsche has usually been thought of as a realist, and at worst, a cynic. But what realist ever talks of the distant future? To the realist, everything is now. And the cynic may speak of the future, but never optimistically. And I might add that in one of his last major concepts, of an "Eternal Recurrence," Nietzsche the "materialist" moved a very great distance toward one of the oldest of theories, Reincarnation. A word of note: The Nietzschean concept of an overman differs markedly from our American idea of a superman. The teutonic concept would be more akin to a high aristocratic type nobility.

Nietzsche had a deep insight into the German character, the like of which few others have ever possessed. He foresaw a future barbarism that in his day was still outwardly invisible. To what extent though Nietzsche's philosophy influenced the development of National Socialism will always remain a subject for debate. Almost surely it had some influence, although many other more immediate and pertinent factors shaped the final course of Nazism. For example, Nietzsche himself was highly erudite as was his creation, Zarathustra. Nazism was not. Nietzsche was not anti-semitic or especially nationalistic. Nazism was both. Yet, in his will to power, and his exemplification of ruthlessness and the great contempt, Nietzsche did lay some groundwork for terrible events to come, whether it was interpreted correctly or not.

The reason I discuss Nazism is because of its strong impact upon history. Hitlerism was a terror, a wild growth, an abnormality—but it possessed a dynamism all its own—easily the most powerful single force our world has ever seen. This is why it is important to recount.

Throughout history there have been all manner of brute tyrannies, but beyond a doubt, Nazi Germany was the proto-type of the ultimate police state. Its philosophy of master race was a world menace, and Hitler was the most dangerous conqueror and tyrant ever to walk this earth. And remember, what the world witnessed and was staggered by were only the early stages of this terrible drama. Though millions were murdered in war and in the extermination camps, Nazism's program of genocide had only just begun. Germany was destroyed, thus the most outlandish, long range plans (the re-location, enslavement, and annihilation of great popula-tions) and eventual control of the world, never had time to emerge! National Socialism was then a catastrophe of unparalleled proportions. As a conquering force it was very successful, to a point—as a cancer is successful. But in every other way it was a failure, from beginning to end. From Rosenberg's demented diatribes to Goebbels' lies to Hitler's diabolical instability—Nazism was a sham. Their entire con-cept of racial superiority was absurd, and what is worse, was contrary to the very ways of modern civilization. In today's world, on any sizeable scale, not only Nazism, but any similar system will not succeed.

It is true, Hitler himself was in some ways our superior—the great spellbinder, invincible conqueror, man of the centuries, philosopher, he was der Fuehrer, he was a com-bination of many things. Yet, this type of supremacy I think to be more in the nature of an aberration, but still within the confines of man, not transcendental. I think that the attempts to deal with Hitler, prior to World War II were justified, even though they failed, because a disastrous war might have been averted. Of course, a militant stand taken at the early stages of his aggression might have been successful. International relations being what they are, however, this is impossible to say. In any event, Churchill, Roosevelt, and Stalin finally proved to be our saviors—for without them, the whole world would have eventually been in chains.

To many, the Nazi SS typified or at least approximated the overman that Nietzsche envisioned. And perhaps it was. I think though that the SS, in Nietzsche's scheme of things, would probably have been a prelude to the overman—"an overture and a going under." In the Nazi scheme of things, it appeared that the SS was being groomed to rule the empire, to be the overman—and that it was the Wehrmacht that was to be the prelude, the "going under." It might be worthy to note however that to Hitler the Reichswehr, the German people, the Nazi Party, even the SS were merely tools to be used toward his special ends. And of them all, he was closest to the party. Probably the SS would have ruled the conquered territories, and attended to some duties within the Reich, but Germany proper would have been ruled and controlled by the Nazi Party.

In any event, the ruler of the territories would have been the lord and master there, the one whose word was law, the new nobility of this earth. And after his time, Hitler would have been looked back upon as something more than a human being. Linz and Berchtesgaden would have been great world shrines, and the day of the Reich would have arrived. But I still do not see how this would have differed appreciably from other nobilities and aristocracies of the past. Perhaps it is a matter of definition, but I still do not see the overman.

It was only after much hesitation that I took the major step of taking issue with Nietzsche. Challenging a super power even in just one echelon, is always dangerous. Were he here to do so, and if he deemed it worth his time, he would undoubtedly cut me down quickly. Be that as it may however, in my opinion a fallacy in Nietzsche's thinking was the qualities of his overman. Nature is brutal, we all know this. Therefore it is a noble concept that man shall be surpassed. And perhaps he shall. But it still remains as to how, in what ways? Needless to say, the Nietzsche concepts of a new barbarism are quite undesirable. Nature has served up enough savagery over the centuries. We need no more of this. Of course one of Nietzsche's reasons for extolling barbarism was his desire to overthrow prevailing powers of that day.

I do not here suggest or even pretend that Nietzsche meant anything other than exactly what he said, and there is much in Nietzsche with which I disagree. A mind with the range and superlative power of Nietzsche's, however, is not easy to understand and sometimes very difficult to interpret. Nietzsche was a hater, but what hater was not once a lover? Nietzsche contradicted himself, but he was almost above contradiction. I think, too, that at times he may have fallen victim (been carried away, as it were) by his own great inspiration—and that at other times he talked theory and abstraction, when his readers thought he meant method and mores that could be applied directly to this life; e.g. Ancient mythology (in which Nietzsche was very learned). Wars and strife among the Deities had little effect upon man.

If a transcendence of man would ever be possible, it would have to come, I think, primarily on the mental side. Were it possible on the physical, muscular side—then this would have occurred long ago, as there have been many human beings with all manner of physical prowess. If it comes it must be on the mental side where the wide horizons for development are. Then perhaps later it may come on the physical side also —through the auspice of human engineering (the new field

32

of genetic study, surgical and biological techniques to improve the efficiency of the human body). But wait, is there not something else—something still lacking?

Principles, high principles and integrity. These attributes, for the most part, are not seen in other forms of life on this earth. Intellectual development alone is not enough, because it can be misused in infernal ways, as for example in war. Brute force is not enough, because the lowest creatures display this. Man is a reasoning creature, thus he is capable of assembling and using thoughts that result in behavior different from any other found upon our planet.

Many are the men who have mis-read history, and interpreted it to mean that since nature is indifferent and cruel, we should also be. This I think is wrong, because—although much of human history is steeped in brutality and violence, we do have qualities that are superior if we but use them. Thus it would follow that more should be expected of us. Instead of emulating nature by being cruel, violent and indifferent, we should try to surpass nature—to surpass man, by being benevolent and interested in the well-being of our fellow men and other creatures. Instead of indifference—compassion. Instead of ruthlessness—persistence, patient persistence against the evil forces of this world—war, disease, corruption, bigotry.

The overman must be above the nature that we know upon this earth. He must manifest qualities that most peoples throughout all of history have regarded as "God like." The ways of the shark are in keeping with the ways of nature on this earth; the ways of the Caesars were in keeping with the ways of nature, as were the ways of Attila, Tamerlane, and Genghis Khan. But the ways of Jesus, of Buddha, of Gandhi, Socrates, Plato, Confucius—these were ways superior to the ways of nature—they transcended the nature of this earth, transcended life as we know it, transcended man. This then

33

was a beginning of the real hierarchy of the superior man.

My own idea of the superior man would be a human being similar to Father Flanagan of world famous Boys Town, or Albert Schweitzer, world renowned medical missionary. Some of the attributes of the superior man must be fearlessness, selflessness, and compassion. He should be peace-loving and non-violent—yet active, not passive, in combatting the major evils of this world. And note, the strongest men in every walk of life are never afraid or ashamed to show compassion. Among human beings, both genders can surpass man, as can the great ones from every race and every nation.

As a positive proof of what is superior, take for example two great opposites—higher education and war. In the case of education there will result all manner of rich rewards: inventions and discoveries to improve life, thought provoking literature, fine music, etc. In the case of war the results are human beings dead, crippled and maimed, whole cities laid waste, vast areas made desolate, people homeless, and nations bankrupt. Can there remain any question as to which is superior and better for mankind? Warriors sometimes claim that non-military civilization becomes corrupt. So does military society. And as to poorer nations becoming jealous of wealthier ones—whenever this occurs they'll have to find other ways to advance rather than the fickle and generally disastrous gambles of war.

Many are the ethical and moral systems of mankind—and most must be considered relative, and at best arbitrary. They are idealistic, with little actual material foundation. Even the questionable and largely outmoded Mosaic Law, which is not idealistic, is nonetheless arbitrary—because whenever it is impossible to reply in kind, then an arbitrary revenge would have to be sought.

Finally, the ways of the superior man must be conditioned upon and based upon the so called Golden Rule, "Do unto others as you would have others do unto you." This maxim is profound in its simplicity, and when followed, the effect that it produces upon human behavior is electric. It is one of the most logical rules in existence and the most ethical—and for most human beings one of the easiest to follow. Psychological deviates, such as sadists and masochists constitute such a small minority that this cannot undermine the law. The Golden Rule is most likely the only ethical law on this earth that has a real material foundation—behavior equated with the self.

SECTION IV

This section deals primarily with everyday life, and will correspond with Chapter V in The New Revolution.

The economic status of the nation and the world is always in a state of change, yet remains basically the same. Work toward earning a livelihood forms the basis for most human activity.

World turbulence today was caused largely by the breakdown of old world empires, the emergence of new nations, new spheres of influence, and the agitation of Communism. The Vietnamese War is the worst tragedy in American history. Several years ago I saw a cartoon in a newspaper, showing the American flag being put through a meat grinder marked "Asia." In addition to our own losses, between the Korean War and the current conflict, we have murdered millions of innocent people. We are interfering in the internal affairs of other countries, and the original purpose is long since past. Even were the war to end tomorrow, we have already lost. Indeed this period will be looked back upon with great shame.

The powerful nation of China must be reckoned with, and we cannot wait much longer. Diplomatic relations of some sort should be established. China has the world's largest population, and the largest standing army. For a private citizen to overlook these facts is foolhardy—for a public official in a policy making position to overlook them or do nothing, is criminal.

By delicate negotiations, a small contingent of troops might safely be stationed in Asia—but if our armed forces continue on a large scale to fight there, eventually it will bring about our ruin. Our country will be financially wrecked, the flower of our youth will be dead or crippled—and if the leaders our people continue to elect still ignore the people's will to end our involvement in these wars—then someday the people may very likely rise up and overthow the government.

The power of the President to dispatch soldiers or technicians throughout the world, should be greatly limited or curtailed. Few other powers have been so abominably abused. A belligerent Democratic President got us into the Korean War. A succession of Presidents have embroiled us in the Vietnamese and Indo-China Wars. These powers turn the President into a dictator and a potential tyrant!

Unlike many, I was against the Vietnam War long before it became a big war and before it became fashionable to oppose it—whereas most of the war opposition developed later when things were going badly. Better late than never, though, that's for sure. Most of the American people now oppose war, unless we are really attacked.

Unfortunately the cowards among us still predominate, as they have in every society in all parts of the world throughout history. They are the followers of the herd, the "yes" men, the parroters of an official line, the lackeys—and they are to be found in every strata of society. They thwart new ideas, and retard and slow progress. They are especially obnoxious in positions of authority, usually in government. Collectively, by the sheer persuasiveness of position, they can make any manner of falsehood appear true. Finally after many years, when the falsehood collapses, they often glibly jump to the other side. This sort of rotten conformity was especially evident in the more than thirty year Democratic rule of the USA, through and after World War II. Wild, fantastic spending and inflation and war preparation were made to appear the new way of life—and its exponents the men of the future.

They were like demented lunatics, whose perverted dream of Pax Americana, was built upon the slain bodies of American boys. It has been said that anything carried to its ultimate extreme becomes absurd. Almost everyone can remember the wild statements by our so called leaders during this insane era—statements often bordering upon madness. "A united America can whip the world" "America can feed the world" "America can easily house the world" "America should police the world" "We are so huge we can do anything" "You never had it so good," etc., etc. The men mouthing these lies should have known better—but either didn't know better, or didn't care. They almost bankrupted the nation before they were finally thrown out. They themselves though became rich. And when the king of the madmen left, he was so hated, that he couldn't run for the office of dog catcher now, and get it.

During this era vast corporate combines came into being, called conglomerates—actual cancers in the economic structure. They were rapacious—selling stocks, bonds, and other toilet paper to the gullible public in order to buy the controlling stock of other companies, often substantial companies. Some conglomerates would then loot these companies of all assets. They were similar to the robber barons of the nineteenth century and the corrupt holding companies of the nineteen-twenties—and fortunately when their puppets in government were thrown out, they too started an immediate decline. This was a stroke of luck for the American people— because had it not occurred, we would all be owned by now.

And the directors of many of the nation's large corporations, men of both political persuasions, often stupid yet bullish, did harm to their own companies and betrayed the stockholders—by their unconscionable extravagance and accrual of debt. This however, did not include charitable causes. If Capitalism had any hope for the future, they all but dashed it. Past leaders such as Andrew Carnegie towered over them. The franchise boom was another "magical" false bonanza, which for many proved to be tantamount to a swindle. Automation is important, but it can also be overdone. It was during this period that clever entrepreneurs around the country organized management seminars—to lure in the suckers, and show the boys out in the sticks how it is done. Together with corrupt zoning boards that would allow three hundred fast food outlets to a city block, if there were room —they ran it into the ground. Toward the end of the franchise bauble, kooky names for the various enterprises began popping up—that could only come out of such places as Los Angeles and New York.

For the first time in almost thirty years the United States has cut back on some military outlays and is combatting monetary inflation. This is a healthy sign, and if continued, should bring about worthwhile results. The military-industrial complex must be brought under control, or it will bankrupt the nation.

There is very great need to raise the living standards of underprivileged people all over the world. Governments can do this if they cut back on armaments. It is remarkable though really that through the long centuries, the human race survived at all—considering the terrible diseases, natural disasters, and wars that have ravaged it. If nothing else, this denotes strength.

The best direction for humanity is still world federal government—and the sooner the better. If not, someday— blooey! Unfortunately there is still a very strong possibility throughout the world for the occasional eruption of small wars. The reasons for this are: absence of an effective world police force—and the fact that the major powers have demonstrated clearly since before World War II and especially after, that they have no intention of entering all out warfare over a dispute involving one small nation. They will send weapons, supplies, and sometimes manpower, and there will be much talk and threats and innuendo, but no large war. With the exception of the danger posed by an unusually strategically located dispute, this tendency should persist for a long time to come. The only way though that war can permanently be ended is disarmament and world government.

Most nations have progressed since World War II. Notable exceptions have been some countries in Latin America, Spain, some of the emerging nations of Africa, a few small nations in Asia, and Israel (the latter's downfall being a very bad choice of location). France, Italy, Russia, West Germany, Japan—all of these nations have shown remarkable progress.

Regarding Soviet Russia, I do not understand the fear that the Communists hold for free speech within their own country. Obviously there are problems inside their borders, just as there are in all other nations—yet their system is established, their people are better off materially than they were in the past, and militarily their country is very strong. What I think they may be overlooking is the fact that historically nations cannot improve themselves significantly without some free thought and speech. In most countries however there is need for some restraint.

Regarding the formation of Israel, the Jews insisted upon pushing into an area already overcrowded, and populated by enemies of very long standing. And this decision was made by Zionist religious fanatics, aided by some corrupt American politicians. Many Jews opposed it, but the fanatics won out. It was like situating your country on the rim of an active volcano. Only a lunatic would do it. And this in turn has accelerated militarism and endangered world peace. Any number of possible choices were available in the vast Pacific area, where no one would or could have bothered them.

41

Jews have done good in the world, but never again should let extremists lead them.

In my opinion the war crime trials in Germany should have ended long ago. Immediately after World War II they were in order, but no more. The point was made and they serve no further worthwhile purpose now—but only cause dissension and discord throughout Germany and the world. This re-opens old wounds and holds West Germany back. The only ones who can benefit are the Communists. East and West Germany should now have the opportunity to develop and progress.

In The New Revolution I said that so far as I am concerned the United States of America is the best country ever. I still believe this. There are though some improvements needed in order to keep it this way and to make it even better. The defense budget should be greatly reduced, and military conscription eliminated. Religion should be allowed only limited power. Federal taxes should be reduced, or if not, then the tax money should be put back into the USA in the form of improvements, environmental cleanup, flood control, etc.

In an economy such as ours, wherein inflation becomes chronic, the government should initiate wage and price controls. Political leaders are usually too cowardly to do this—but this is what should be done. The government already controls our lives in ways more serious than this (and contrary to our best interests)—so why can't they initiate a program that would help us, that would help the entire American people? If some of the large manufacturers and large labor unions oppose this, that's too bad. They've had their way long enough.

I have always been a friend to organized labor (and they have done much to help all of us), however there is something, said before, that I think bears repeating. In our country

42

the labor unions have forced their wages too high. This has helped fuel monetary inflation and has done private enterprise, the American people, and our country considerable harm. To a substantial extent this has caused the prices of American products to become exorbitant, thereby being continually undersold on the world market. And within our country the people and industry must pay these outlandish prices for our own products, or buy imports that are lower in price. More often than not they purchase the foreign imports. The many taxes on our products contribute to this also. In time this will close many American factories, and has already contributed to the balance of payments deficit. Nations could, I think, greatly reduce the harm from these deficits by selective use of the barter system.

As the country reduces its military budget, and unemployment increases—the federal government should initiate vast programs within the country of: cleanup of environmental pollution, flood control, bridge and road building, railway improvement, etc. Such programs can employ millions of people for many years, and would be money well spent. When the economy grows stronger again these people could then be gradually absorbed back into private industry. The governmental programs should be similar to the WPA of depression years, only on a much larger scale.

There is some waste within every program, this is to be expected. If some workers loaf on the job, this is unfortunate but it cannot be entirely eliminated. The main factor is that the money would be spent within our own country for the benefit of our own people—whereas in military spending most of the money goes into a few industrial pockets or overseas to be mis-appropriated by an elite few, and the remainder in the form of munitions blown up. The poor people over there don't receive it anyway. Of course, various other countries that have had a twenty-five year free ride at the American taxpayer's expense—are quick to tout the need for "collective security," which incidentally never existed during this period anyhow.

I think that general disarmament holds far more promise of success in preventing war, than mere nuclear limitation. I still believe that the most effective way of achieving world disarmament would be for the major countries to turn in their weapons gradually to the United Nations. The armed forces of the world organization should be completely international in character and under international command. As the individual nations become militarily weaker, the world organization would grow continually stronger. In this way an overall disarmament could in time be enforced. Unfortunately, connivance and intrigue exist within nations and between nations. A world government can however minimize its effects by remaining alert.

Next to military disarmament, world population control is the most important problem today. Over the centuries mankind was fruitful and multiplied—and polluted the world—not to mention the multitudinous other ills that he caused. Beyond any doubt, mass starvation looms not far ahead unless the upward spiral of population growth is checked. The argument so often used against birth control, that the land surfaces of the earth are still largely empty, is based upon a half truth, and the argument is false. Much of the earth's surface is still uninhabited, as the bulk of the human race is clustered in more favorable areas and concentrated in cities and towns. But most of the earth is either covered by water or by today's standards uninhabitable.

Individual companies can build a few model towns, and governments could probably develop some of these areas, however it would all be very costly. And to induce people to migrate there would be harder still. High premiums would have to be paid to promote such homesteading. Civilization, as we know it, is set up as we see it, was thus established hundreds of years ago, and is today thoroughly dependent upon this structure. Industry and commerce could not successfully or profitably function in widely scattered, remote and desolate areas. Transportation, power, resources, people—none of these would be available in large enough quantities. The natural elements would be more difficult to overcome—and the world's economic system, never too hardy, might very likely suffer a relapse into deep recession. In short, except in isolated situations, all of the combined technology on earth cannot change this, and can only alter it over a long period of time. Such a re-distribution would take centuries—whereas the population crisis is now. Birth control is the major answer—and secondly, development of new types of emergency foods, such as molds, yeasts, algaes, etc.

As science continues to advance, large populations will become more and more of a liability. Not only do they drastically reduce the quality of life, but in the long run even undermine and weaken the quantity, the basic strength and drive essential to life. And militarily their value is even questionable.

I will cite an example to clarify the point. I knew of a residential neighborhood—better than average, clean, land-scaped, it had a well cared for look. One time a couple moved into the area, bringing with them a number of children, six or eight. Immediately trouble began. The children began annoying their neighbors—running and throwing things into their yards, being loud, boisterous, etc. Complaining was to no avail. Very soon the neighbor on one side moved. In less than six months their other neighbor did the same. By now the properties were becoming difficult to sell, so in due time another couple with a large family of children moved in. About two years later I had occasion to drive through the neighborhood again, and now it was hardly recognizable. Trash and debris most everywhere, a number of for sale signs were now up, there was very little grass or shrubbery left, and most of the outside yard lamps had been broken. The children that I saw were ragged and appeared undernourished, and a pack of vicious looking dogs roamed about freely.

For those diminishing few who, despite the ugly plight of our world, still tout the irresponsible cycle of childbearing— I might remind why governments wanted more people. For cannon fodder, more meat for the slaughterhouse of war— and why the Pope still wants more children—to pay his salary and those of his subordinates, enhance his power, and buy new ornaments for his vast cathedrals.

America's society today is in a state of agitation and ferment. The major antagonism between blacks and whites in America will eventually subside—although this will be several decades away. In time the extremist, splinter groups, both black and white, should decline—as they constitute only a very small minority of the people.

Violent crime will also be greatly reduced, as race relations improve, and if military conscription is ended. The avalanche of narcotic and hallucinatory drugs will also decline. Force alone though cannot stop crime. Simplification of court procedures, and possibly some degree of legal immunity from being sued, might remove some of the obstacles that prevent people from coming to the aid of others and getting involved.

Also it is worthy to note that sex crimes can be greatly reduced if prostitution would be sanctioned—and if it were legalized and taxed, venereal disease would decline. It is also an aid in population control. Almost without exception, in countries of the world where prostitution is tolerated, women are safe on the streets alone, day or night. Several nations, wherein in a flurry of false ideals, prostitution was outlawed, are even now considering its reinstatement.

A large amount of police effort and resources are wasted today against so called "vice"—whereas it should be directed instead against serious crimes, street violence, robberies, burglaries, assaults, etc. And a re-codification of all laws, and scrapping of outmoded laws is badly needed throughout the United States—and undoubtedly someday this will be done. Almost every Bar Association and legal group favor this.

In the early days of the Republic the pioneer spirit did much to hold the nation together. Also, we were not involved in foreign wars then. I think that the main cause for the troubles that beset us today is our continuous involvement in foreign wars since early in this century. The greatest of our founders warned against this. And until this continuous involvement in curtailed, I do not think that our problems can be solved. Disengagement from foreign conflicts would give our nation the opportunity to develop normally again.

Military conscription should be eliminated, as it is a threat to our very way of life. It undermines and disrupts every aspect of young people's lives, and is extremely harmful to higher education. And it is upon higher education that much of our nation's future depends.

The young people of America in their desire to improve the world are trying to break out of old patterns and ways of doing things, that have had their day and are now failing. There will be many awkward starts and stops, but the endeavor is worthwhile.

We should be receptive to new ideas—because things are not static, and the world is in a constant state of change. I recall a Mauldin newspaper cartoon that showed a man with an American flag draped over his head and body so that he could not see, and he seemed to be groping about as would a blind man. On the front of the flag was a little placard that read "obedience is patriotism." Another man standing alongside commented "It was designed as a flag, Buddy—not as a blindfold." There is a great deal of truth in this. Honest dissent is essential to the maintenance of freedom, in fact freedom cannot long endure without it.

The disorder on the nation's campuses was ignited by the Vietnam War. If and when the United States disengages itself from foreign wars, campus disorder should gradually subside.

Many of today's young people feel ungrateful toward prior generations, and this is unfortunate. True, there is much that is wrong with the world, but also there has been a good deal accomplished. We should try to give youth aid and advice, however should not expect them to heed much of the advice. This is sad, but it seems that each generation must learn some lessons themselves, the hard way.

Many young people have made fools of themselves in their use of narcotics—much as their elders have done in their overindulgence in alcohol. I advise against the use of hallucinatory drugs and narcotics, as well as the overindulgence in alcohol. There is entirely too much alcohol in the American way of life today. This crosses all social, economic lines, and includes people of every political persuasion. A few years ago it was excess smoking, and tens of thousands went to early graves as a result. Now it is drinking—and it is generally known and acknowledged by the highest authorities that excess alcohol is harmful—physically, morally, and mentally. In the long run, I think that it is more harmful than tobacco.

To young extremists I say this: Stay away from violence. Turn your energies toward politics—it will get you farther. Violence can bring change, but it is far more likely to bring tyranny than freedom.

As a whole, the hipster movement has been very good for young people. It has given them a sense of purpose, and the desire to accomplish worthwhile things. It's just that a small minority of bad apples, such as exist in every group, have made it harder for the rest.

There have been martyrs among today's youth, particularly those who died or were imprisoned fighting military conscription. There are some older citizens too, who sacrificed established careers, toward this end. These are great people —and this never should be forgotten.

Some modern heroes among the young today are—the Beatles, Bob Dylan, The Rolling Stones, Joan Baez, Jane Fonda, Johnny Cash, Donovan, some of the Black militants, etc. They are not always the deepest of thinkers, but they are usually altruistic, often heroic and know what the young people want.

There is a wide misunderstanding on the part of youth today regarding financial interests. These interests are basic to our society, yet since the late nineteen-thirties they have been debased by becoming closer and closer linked to the war making system. In World War II this was a necessity, but since that time it is very unfortunate. Usually the banks have been only indirectly involved, for it is the industrialists who manufacture armaments for the government who are generally the criminals. The uncaring industrialists or their representatives approach the banks for loans and other financial services. True, the banks have often been willing, sometimes eager to extend their aid, and have profited thereby. They were not, though, the instigator. Naturally they should have resisted and brought pressure to bear, politically, socially, etc., in order to slow the trend toward militarism. Unfortunately they did not. But bear in mind that it was not always this way, and may not always remain this way. Prior to the thirties the banks in our country were not identified with militarism, because there

wasn't much militarizing then. They have always been identified with the status quo, but it is the U. S. militarism that has
inflamed our youth with anti-military hatreds, nihilism, and
sometimes in desperation, even anti-Americanism. There is
though a trend in the business world today, away from militarism—and this may have some very important influence
upon the future.

Youth in Russia and China will, I suppose, continue to
incline toward an uncritical patriotism—though from what
I have read I would think that in time they will demand more
liberalization. In America, whatever course a substantial
portion of youth pursues, will generally be chosen on a less
rational basis than in many other places. The reason for this
is that religion, a brief encounter with liberalism, capitalism,
and militarism have so distorted their views and ideas—that
there is no way of foretelling what direction they may go.
The hipster movement has though been generally good for
youth, because it is a serious movement and involves attain-
able, tangible goals.

The use of narcotics, on the other hand, has been an
irrational phenomenon, and the minority who gravitated in
that direction are immature. Where these same youths will
gravitate next is impossible to say. Some might arm themselves and become militants of the far left or far right. If
others would perchance latch onto the fervor of a religious
dogma (which is the ancient catch-all for the irrational)—
only harm can result. Because next to narcotics, there is
nothing else weaker than this.

The sexual freedom that is manifest today is good for the
country. It represents the expression of a deep seated urge
that was frustrated for many decades. You hear all sorts of
dire predictions regarding this, but they are wrong. Sex is a
great power in this world and should not be unduly thwarted.
If it is, the effects can be very dangerous. The social pen-

dulum though is always moving back and forth, so we may expect it to move again toward the right. This is natural, no doubt as a part of human stability—however the trend should not be allowed to swing too far to the right or remain there very long—because this is the reactionary, regressive side of man. Basically people are reactionary. It is only after they've been aroused that they become revolutionary—and even then they soon lapse back into a pattern that is reactionary. Man is largely a crisis creature.

We hear a great deal nowadays about the far left and far right. There is good and bad in every group, and the far right is no exception. In addition to psychotics, there is also some very fine, stalwart virtue there. Unfortunately taken as a whole, the far right of every country is reactionary toward change, therefore an obstacle in the path of progress, and must be opposed. In America the far right is composed largely of Birchers, Kluxers and their kind. In Soviet Russia the forces of reaction are largely the Communist Party itself. Throughout the world the forces of reaction are almost invariably committed either to status quo of the present, or to the past.

The far left, too, is dangerous, as it is composed of various militants. Some of them are violent and uncompromising, others irrational and nihilistic. And all of the extremes abhor the sane middle ground. Possible benefits might be gained if some of the extremes could be lured back into the mainstream of mankind. Incidentally, the far right and the military can never bring us law and order, such as they boast —at least not the type law and order that you want. Force can be useful at times, but pushed to its ultimate, it becomes self-defeating. Their type law and order would be more akin to the death squads of Brazil and the terrible massacres of Vietnam.

Remember there is always a potential menace from the

far right and the deep South. The southern states have harbored a bitter grudge for over one hundred years—unjustified because they were wrong in the first place. Politically they form the balance of power between the two major parties—and if ever they should elect one of their states' rights people to the Presidency, that would most likely be the end of our freedom. They would set us back many decades, and a great amount of hard won progress would be lost. This menace does not emanate from all of the southern states, but centers mostly around those that formed the hard core of the Confederacy. Also, many individuals throughout the entire South, both white and black, would love to progress and throw off the shackles of hatred from out of the past—but the political power structure there holds them back. The military-industrial complex has done much to strengthen the South and make it more aggressive—by awarding them an excessively large amount of defense contracts. There are several interesting similarities between our southern states and southern Germany. They too were poorer than the north, and were the hotbed of Nazism. The U. S. federal government should remove many of its war contracts from the south, thus reducing their power and menace.

What the moralists and censors have always been too thickheaded to understand is that a great many people want the right to read or see or do this or that—and they want to know that they can do it. This does not necessarily mean that they will do it. In fact very often once a person knows that he can—that it is no longer forbidden, the desire diminishes. Anything that is forbidden takes on a new allure. For example, were it forbidden to expose the arms to view—immediately this would become a hush-hush subject, secretive, tantalizing, causing furtive glances, giggles. Were it forbidden to drink tea, immediately a whole new lore would be born, and a blackmarket appear, fed by an ever growing underground of innuendo and propaganda. This would make tea drinking appear alluring, sinful, obscene, dangerous, and far more delicious than it really is.

Monogamy is superior to polygamy—but a monogamy with fewer sexual restraints and religious stupidities. I am not in favor of communal living, whether it is for adults or children. In The New Revolution I stated a preference for it, for two reasons. First, I felt that it had merit. Since then I have changed my mind. Sex between single people and even between swinging couples is in order, but they do not usually live together. Secondly, I used it as a battering-ram against some of the false morality that prevailed then. I no longer favor communal living, because the individual loses his identity here. Also, though most individuals do not keep themselves and their surroundings as clean as they might—when thrown together in a group, their dirtiness is compounded, and soon, pigs would even leave to seek out more wholesome quarters. Of course where people must live together, as in institutions, that is another matter. Even then however things should be as individualized as possible.

So far as the various psychoses of modern civilization are concerned, we make some of our own problems. Remember, the early settlers of our land did not have many nervous problems—because they didn't have time for them! I think though that human beings will always have some moral dilemmas to face. To kill or not to kill, to lie or not to lie, to help or not to help, to procreate or not to procreate, etc. And then too, our own body functions present some dilemmas, e.g. the unpleasantness and embarrassment regarding excrement and flatulence, and the health hazard posed by the former. These are dilemmas that we are forced to live with.

In our country today there is a strong resurgence of interest in the subjects of witchcraft, soothsaying, etc. This can be beneficial, so long as it is not carried to extremes.

Restoration of historical homes has already gotten underway throughout our country, and the interest in antiquities is probably at an all time high. These are I think healthy trends, because they should help restore some of the balance to human life—where the sterility of modern architecture has obliterated it. As is well known regarding our modern highway network—the freeway, expressway, inter-state systems are very complex, difficult, and monotonous. I have one modest suggestion to make in this respect. The use of a different color on signs and markers for major turnoffs might be of help.

In America today life in the smaller towns is still rather tranquil. Of course for the larger cities the tempo must be faster. In the cities themselves there has been a strong trend for many years toward the suburbs. Also it might be worthy of note, a small but growing number of young executives who have been deserting the corporate complex, for simpler lives.

A considerable amount of American television programming is, in my opinion, harmful to the nation. I refer particularly to the super spy shows and some westerns. They foster violence, disrespect for law, and great recklessness— most of it sheer fantasy. I hate to think how many youngsters have been injured and killed imitating these things—and no doubt a few adults.

Women have made great advances in the past fifty years. Today and in the future they will make more large advances. They should realize of course that in coming into very nearly full competition with men, they will have to forfeit certain privileges that have been theirs for long periods of time. They will gradually become subject to certain diseases engendered by economic pressures and job hazards, heretofore almost exclusively affecting men. They may also have to fight in war, something that they have rarely done before.

54

Nonetheless they will advance. I do not think though that they should try to supplant men. Those fools who downgraded the fine art of homemaking, did our society a great deal of harm. A well managed, congenial homelife is important—as today's delinquency and broken marriages amply demonstrate. Each sexual gender has its own unique qualities and functions, created by nature and established in and ingrained into the living patterns of humanity over thousands upon thousands of years.

Each sex will gradually take on some of the duties of the other, sharing certain obligations that heretofore were the province of just one. This is happening today, and will no doubt prove of benefit to society, so long as it does not go to extremes. Women have also done considerable good in the peace movement (something that they seldom did in the past)—and by uniting their efforts they can further other worthwhile causes in the future. There is of course a small but vocal extremist element within the women's liberation movement—much as there is in every group of human beings. The extremists want always to rule or ruin, and seem determined to undermine the good work that others have done.

In any relatively free society there is almost certain to be some amount of turmoil. Several years ago though an outstanding American said words to the effect that he does not think that "in America we have a race problem—but instead a race agitator problem." More recently the Vice-President was reputed to have said that "The hidden cause of malaise in America is the success of the American system. . . . When a man who has had nothing, gets something, his natural impulse is not to be humbly thankful, but to want more—that's human nature." There is a great deal of truth in both of these statements. And the President himself counseled us to lower our voices. If ever we reach the point wherein at least a nominal amount of concern and respect are felt and shown by the people for one another, then much more order will prevail and the country will grow stronger.

Religion should, I think, continue to play some part in American life—however never should be allowed to re-assert its power of yesteryear—for that was obnoxious, puerile, and suffocating. The virulent disease known as Evangelism or fundamentalism has always been especially disgusting—and has since time immemorial been a haven for the gullible, the lunatic, and those about ready for the asylum. And the corrupt politicians with their prayer breakfasts—I could tell you something about these. Of course politicians have always touted religion for their own selfish ends. They no doubt need the prayer—to salve a guilty conscience. It is much easier to pray for something, free of effort, or go through the motions of praying—than it is to go out and actually work toward its attainment. And as to the ones who are praying for guidance—the only guidance that most politicians are interested in is how to steal more money from the voters and taxpayers, and how to be re-elected. If the Almighty ever really did listen to any of the hot air issuing from these jackals, He'd probably laugh in their faces!

Basically, religion has strength, we all know this. The trouble is that its strength and energies have usually been misdirected. Had their efforts over the centuries been against war instead of vice, we probably would not be at the edge of disaster today. In the past and up until very nearly the present, society wanted religion to give its rubber stamp approval and blessings to everything those in power did. This was the way of life for hundreds of years. Society wanted dogma and ritual, because that is not religion. This was another facet of exploitation by the great money interests, that similarly exploit politics. At last though religion is beginning to assert itself and oppose war, bigotry, and corruption—which is a big step and is all to the good.

Organized religion today should try to divest itself of its superstitions, and throw out most of its dogma and ritual, not all of it, but most of it—in other words, downgrade the fairytales. Most of the human race are too mature for this now anyhow. This ancient language of error does nothing but divide and enslave mankind, and in the long run weakens religion. The churches have a long tradition of dogma and ritual, and many will claim that this is the cohesive force that has held them together. This was true of the past, but is no longer true in the present. And in the future, dogma and ritual will be the greatest of liabilities. An extremely small percentage of people favor ritual and perhaps even need it. But for the vast majority, dogmas and ritual are the worst of troublemakers. It has always been thus, that whenever men try to describe in detail the hereafter, and name the attributes of the Ultimate—that is when they get into trouble. Disposing of dogma and ritual would be a purging, a purification which in the long run would have valuable results. Many of today's religious leaders favor this.

Humanity in general should try to rid itself of most superstition and prejudice, as these hold man back. Many oddities though that are often popularly classed as superstition, have a solid basis. Thus, efforts should be made to separate one from the other. Prayer should be kept out of the public schools, and the lofty barriers between church and state jealously guarded.

I think that religion of the future should retain a slender tie with mysticism, providing a place for meditation, etc., because spiritual belief is superior to materialism—but should concentrate its major efforts on peace, race problems, and welfare. Clerics of the future should divest themselves of most ritual and dogma—and leave these to just the relatively few theologians who spend their full time with mysticism. In this way both groups would benefit. The larger group could accomplish more benevolent work, by being unburdened of ritual, which they never did effectively—and the smaller group, by being relieved of social commitments, could delve deeper into religious mysticism. And there are powers and values to be gotten from mysticism (prayer included) for the relatively few adept in the field.

"He ain't heavy, Father . . . he's m' brother." This motto from Boys Town should, in my opinion, become a watchword of the future. But philanthropy in the years ahead should differ from that of the past, in that charity should begin at home. Emergency aid, always, to people anywhere—but only after the major problems in our own country are solved should we send continuing aid abroad.

Generally speaking, the large majority of legislators throughout our country, in state legislatures and in the U. S. Congress, comprise the lower elements in our society. There are of course some honest and excellent legislators, however they are always in the minority and can do little. Occasionally they do accomplish some good works, but this is seldom. The majority of law makers, in the beginning, are slightly above the average population in ability and experience—but where they perpetually fail is by their cowardice—they fear the disapproval of their constituents so much that they refuse to do what they usually know to be correct. The most that their constituents can do is to vote them out at the next election—but these legislators are so greedy to hold office that they would rather sell the country down the river than chance losing some popularity. Sometimes they would even gain popularity by doing what is right, but they are afraid to risk it. Another cause for bad legislation are payoffs—however the vast majority of cases are caused by cowardice alone. The law makers in Washington refuse to trim the military budget. In the name of patriotism they will drown the nation in an overdose of debt. Payoffs are often the cause here. It is their fault too that the President has become a dictator. The law makers in state legislatures, pass blue laws. Cowardice and stupidity are usually the cause here. Lumped together, these men are low, low by their own choice and doing, lower than the scum that roam our alleys. I hate to have to say this about so important an element of our society, but unfortunately it is true.

Some of the Southern politicians who give their all toward perpetuating' everything that is bad—eventually their own descendants will look back upon them as a disgrace. And those members of the U. S. House of Representatives and U. S. Senate, in general, who vote continually to increase military spending and refuse to end military conscription (even though these evils will ruin us)—and who have continually given their backing to our involvement in far away wars, conflicts that add nothing whatever to our own security, but instead seriously weaken our country—is it not possible that at least a few of them may actually be Communist agents, saboteurs—planted by Moscow, over a period of years, in order to ruin us. Remember, this type of connivance has happened many times before in world history.

I regret even to have to state this, but I think that Communism will become dominant throughout most of the world, in the far future. The reason does not constitute a testimonial to the virtues of Lenin. It is simply the fact that the majority of people throughout the world are still very poor, and their ancestors were exploited by monarchies for thousands of years. In the last couple of centuries they were exploited by capitalism. There is a legacy of hate here, and what I think the people as a whole will gradually turn to will be the movement, the rudiments of which even the uneducated can comprehend and conform to, a system that provides and regiments, exacts vengeance, enforces law, and is materialistic—namely Communism. I would be sorry to see it, but I think that this is the way it will be.

The economies of the Capitalist countries are too erratic, self-centered, and subject to monetary storms and depressions, to be able to solve the large problems of the world. Thus, in the longer run, it can only be done by slow, steady, plodding, stumbling, human, all too human Communism and Socialism.

In addition to reducing the scope of human freedom, the Communist world has done another thing yet worse. With its materialism, it offers the people only one final ending, oblivion. Since its materialistic theory is wrong, the millions of lives that it darkens, is indeed a crime. I might remind the Communists, that historically the peoples of the earth have generally been more willing to endure hardships, when they hold a belief in the hereafter. Such a belief could be re-established easily enough, minus dogma and ritual which are stupid and dangerous. If ever this were done, it should be simple, streamlined, and probably re-named, e.g. "We have come to the conclusion that there is an afterlife for all, that is both better and wider in range. Beyond this, nothing further is known by man." This might be called "Communist Realization."

The masses of humanity are still largely uneducated and economically poor—but there are a great many of them, spread throughout the world. With modern technology at their service, which it will be, they will advance. Man for man they could not overcome the more affluent nations, but with their vast preponderance of numbers they are certain to eventually prevail. The coarse, heavy, vulgar will gain mastery. The uneducated peasant will hardly appreciate the finer cultures he has supplanted—but this theme has been repeated many times throughout history.

The decline of Capitalism, though certain, may become slower as it becomes more socialized. Within another century, however, socialism and communism will dominate most of the world. The USA will hold a place in the future, but probably will not remain entirely capitalistic.

Socialism, I regard as being the most advanced human system, such as we see in the Netherlands today. And it is very possible that by being chosen by more and more of the emerging nations—it will be socialism that will dominate the distant future. Conditions on this earth being what they are, however, I am inclined to think that it will be the coarser, harder communism that will prevail. Too much fanaticism, however, on the part of the communists could undermine their chances. Freedom will gradually emerge again, however, much as the breaking through of perennial flowers—and some will persist in the future. The condition of the world ahead, will be that long coming harvest, that thousands of years of oppression have wrought, i.e. Edwin Markham's "The Man With the Hoe."

The only notable alteration I can see in this projection of the future would be if there comes another world war. In that event, what remains of civilization would be ruled by scattered tyrannies, communism among them. Any uncommitted nations which might escape direct destruction, would emerge as strong forces, at least for the time. They too however would suffer to a lesser or greater extent from the war's side effects—radioactive poisoning, biological plagues, widespread poverty, etc. Even then the possibility for world government might emerge again—but if there is not a great war, then the idea of world government should grow continually stronger as the years go by. Another factor that adds to this probability is that World War II was very likely the last great war of outright conquest that our civilization will ever know.

Liberal altruism should be the way of the future. As things stand yet today, Humanism, The American Civil Liberties Union, and churches such as the Unitarian and Society of Friends would be the most suitable elements to lead the way. And undoubtedly they will play a significant role well into the future. But since the forces of liberalism, in general, display somewhat less stability than might be desired—then for the long pull, the major churches, liberalized, both Protestant and Catholic, would I think be the more ideal vehicle for forging ahead—and on a world scale major religions such as Hindu and Buddhism. The religions combined still form the bulk of the human race. Other than Communism, there is nothing else to equal this. Most human beings need a certain amount of discipline imposed upon them, as they seem to lack ample discipline of their own. In The New Revolution I voiced the opinion that, as things stand, a limited democracy or republic would probably be more successful and durable than total freedom. The Catholic church in particular has the structural backbone and organization suitable for this, and if liberalized, could do a vast amount of good in the world. Dogma and ritual, however, must be reduced, or the churches cannot succeed. Though Communism and Socialism will dominate the far future—there will still be many parts of the world and areas of life where enlightened religion can carry on successfully and do much good.

One of the worst dangers facing our country today is the gun lobby. This is an immediate and insidious problem. A very large percentage of our citizens are armed, some of them heavily. This is extremely dangerous, already causes all sorts of killings, and can bring about multiple murders, massacres, assassinations, kidnappings, and insurrections. All guns should be registered and licensed, maybe even taxed—and no one should be permitted to own an arsenal.

It is interesting to note that one of the same arguments

62

used by gun enthusiasts to justify their madness, has also been used by those opposed to the licensing and regulation of motor vehicles, and driving safety rules. Needless to say, as dangerous as our streets are, they would be many times worse were it not for regulation. Originally the opponents of Pure food and drug laws also used the same type of arguments that the gun enthusiasts use today. In a society of people, there must be some rules, or everything disintegrates.

One other word I want to say on this. At a public gathering once, I heard several National Rifle Assn. followers say to one another that they were considering bringing before their group a proposal that lobbying be started in the U. S. Congress for repeal of all firearms laws—so that everyone could carry a weapon of any kind, much as it was in the days of the old west. Surely the American people will not allow this to happen—not allow themselves to be led to ruin this way.

Before I close this section I want to voice a final warning regarding the danger of militarism. There is no question that in lieu of an effective world government, and with enemies in the world, we need some amount of national defense. But, as I discussed in The New Revolution, this does not mean that we should panic. The type defense program our country has been on for the past two decades, can only lead to our bankruptcy and destruction. A sensible and effective defense posture is however possible.

Even though the Pentagon has grown unpopular throughout the USA because of their bungling of the Vietnamese War, the thousands of our young men they lost, the atrocities they committed, the disgrace they brought upon our nation, and the propagandizing and spying they have done upon our own people—they are still dangerous, and unless checked, could gain control of our country. The avenue by which they can accomplish this is by monopolizing the federal budget.

They already get most of it! If they steadily increase their percentage of the budget, year after year—in not too long a time they and their industrial allies, and the various political criminals in Congress, whom they control, will be too powerful to stop. They will then take over the nation. That would be the end of our freedom. Remember, militarism is a disease that has ruined and destroyed most all of the nations and empires of this earth throughout all of history!

In this section I shall discuss liberalism, the press, critics, universities, and other selected subjects.

I have learned this about liberals. Taken as a group, their ideals place them at the very forefront of humanity. But as individuals many of them are sadly lacking. They drink too much liquor and are not always as intellectual and liberal as they claim. I have been disappointed with the liberals. Many of them are divorcees and incline toward Hedonism and sensualism. Taken alone, these facts would not be impressive—because human beings are human beings the world over. In the case of liberals however, they are usually better educated than average and generally hold higher ideals—thus more should be expected of them.

I am reminded too of the people who think up or at least parrot so called sophisticated words, actual stupidities that we are forced to hear over and over again. Such dandies as "posh, escalate, expertise, charisma, zany, nitty-gritty, hang-up," etc., etc. These cocktail party bums and hangers on, found in every major city, and of both political spectrums—are at best, of little value to mankind. Sometimes also known as polite society, they might better be called "stupid society." I cringe when I think of what future generations will do to these low, moronic witticisms—they'll deal with them in a similar manner, no doubt, to what our generation did to such vermifuges as "twenty-three-skidoo," and "boop-oop-a-doop."

Regarding the American press I want to say that for the most part they still display prejudice. A good example of this, selected at random, occurred during the latter years of Democratic rule in the nineteen sixties. The lackeys of the news media, social climbing drunkards, stated dutifully (not as was correct, that the economy was rotten with corruption and ready to collapse), but instead that "the economy is overheated." Another example concerned an American political leader who was assaulted unmercifully by the press for years, particularly when he was down. The news media virtually outdid one another to see who could kick him the hardest. When finally he fooled them all, and returned from his political grave to become President—this strange prejudice disappeared, and now they act as if they knew his true worth all along! Amazing isn't it?

I want to say something regarding critics. In many instances their power has been abused. This is particularly true of the better known critics writing for large newspapers and magazines. There was a play on Broadway one time that was a hit. It had good reviews most of the way. The play had a clever title, but was otherwise low budget trash, a piece of nothing with few redeeming qualities. It wasn't obscene. It wasn't anything, except perhaps a fake. During each performance, some patrons were seen to walk out. Yet the critics continued to heap praises upon the producer, as if he were some sort of tin god—and as a result the play made money and continued to run. On his next venture, however, which everyone thought would be so great, the sun did not shine! This play was a tremendous flop, and closed after a short while. Several old timers told me afterward that they thought he had paid off a key critic on the first one, but mistakenly thought that he no longer needed them and refused to pay off the second time.

About fifteen years ago a book came out on the subject of special education. Around the same time, another book was issued by a different publisher, concerning a fictional female with loose morals, who spent most of her time in bed with men. I never read one major review about the book on special education—but the critics couldn't seem to say enough regarding the woman with loose morals, and of course it became a best seller. Today, there is scarcely a person anywhere who can even remember the name of the book about the harlot, let alone its lack-luster story—but the book on special education is known in many quarters, and has influenced teaching methods throughout many parts of the world.

Most public libraries I have found to be very satisfactory, and most librarians quite capable and dedicated. Just a few of the latter, though, I found to be lacking, mostly in courage of their convictions. Public libraries form such an important bulwark in a democratic society, that it is essential they remain free. Libraries should be havens for free-thought, and bow to no would be censor or special interests.

Universities too are in an unparalleled position with regard to man's future, and the advancement of civilization. Education today is a complex business, and most houses of learning are doing reasonably well, in terms of the situation. Some however can stand special improvements. Some departments seem allergic to new ideas, and philosophy departments I found often to be reactionary. More often than not they are bound up on method (method is more important to science than philosophy), and forget that many of humanity's greatest achievements have been wrought by men of modest means, and have come through unconventional methods and techniques differing from those favored or approved at a given time. Moreover, philosophers whom they revere, and whose word they bank upon each day, in their own time, could not even gain admission to many of the leading universities.

We need technical studies in profusion, and of many different types, in order to advance. But few of the great books of history have been technical studies—and fewer still of the technical works have been among books that have inspired and led men. The great books have most always been of the type that have captured and presented the spirit or essence of an idea—punctuated with some degree of emotion.

I for one could have played it safe, easily enough—and simply reiterated philosophies out of the past, familiar ground that has been trodden over thousands of times. But had I done this there would have been no point in philosophizing at all, as we hardly need more of the same. And of course it always holds true that those who do not venture forth, seldom make mistakes. But they don't do anything innovative either. Were most people like this, we'd still be living in straw huts.

Also, the philosophies of complacency, sometimes called peace of mind, even Existentialism, are incorrect on this point. It does matter what we do—even at the very least, because without the exercise of some degree of conscience, people are forced into conformity and drawn into mass movements, thereby often unwittingly aiding in the commission of all manner of crimes.

Some college pedants may have looked askance at my work, because it was not formalized, and discussed subjects "beneath their dignity"—and because I never sought formal admittance to the faculties of their ivy covered tombs; and perhaps because I never tossed around the name of a certain Dutchman, a little pseudo-intellectual game of name dropping so fashionable several years ago. But allow me to tell them this: Your little critiques of pure reason and shining syllogisms would not last five minutes outside of your little sheltered world. The battles of life are not fought according to the Marquis of Queensberry Rules. The brawling smoke-blackened panorama of life—politics, commerce, war—these dominant factors would make mincemeat out of you.

And last but not least let me mention certain literary

circles that are not all they might be. These are the ones, principally women's groups, wherein it once was so popular to mention the name of a certain English poet, then giggle. Many more of the social type women's clubs fancy themselves as being quite cultured, with their innocuous little book reviews and afternoon teas. A number of these women are themselves amateur writers and artists. Unfortunately they are sure to remain amateur. Their idea of culture might be a bit of "Pilgrims Progress"—and "Lovely as a Tree" would be about as controversial a work as they would dare program.

SECTION VI

This section will correspond generally with Chapter IV Part 3, of The New Revolution. Since 1963, year of The New Revolution, humanity has sent numerous vehicles into outer space and has set foot upon the moon. Vast progress will be made in the future in many fields, such as space exploration, electronics, computer technology, physics, micro-biology, surgery, and even parapsychology.

In The New Revolution I spoke out against certain phases of commercial aviation. There were two reasons for this. First I wanted to disperse some of the hypocrisy of that period. During the nineteen-fifties there were bomb scares on passenger aircraft—and instead of taking effective measures to prevent explosives from being brought or sent aboard, they made it virtually illegal to say the word "bomb." Secondly, I underestimated the subsequent technological progress that the aircraft industry has made. I was wrong about this. Regarding the future of transportation I would say that air travel will be the major means in the eras to come. This should prevail, until such a time that it too may be surpassed. In a more immediate sense, the automobile will play an important role, and possibly an updated railway system.

Surgical spare parts techniques of the future will push the human life span well beyond what it is today. As science advances, the differences between man and machine will narrow—until eventually they may become as one, or finally machines may evolve into a new race! One of the potentially greatest fields will I think be the field of human engineering —the study of improving the efficiency of the human body through surgical, biological, and other means. This bold venture into uncharted fields may ultimately have vast implications—and the names of the men who pioneered it through this century will be elevated and revered.

In America consumer protection has been established—and at long last the human race has awakened to the dangers of excess population growth and environmental pollution. The tasks ahead in these areas are vast and of long duration. Our rivers and streams and lakes have become sewers. The air we breathe is no longer clean, and even as large a body as the ocean is becoming contaminated. Destruction of environment has been going on steadily throughout the world for centuries. This indisputable fact in itself is a good indication of the magnitude of the problem. Excess growth of population and industrialization during the nineteenth and twentieth centuries have greatly compounded the problem.

Numerous thinkers, over a long span of time, have voiced concern over environmental pollution—but the populace as a whole and their debauched and corrupted leaders would not listen. In the United States we have lost twenty good years since World War II, during which time much could have been done to clean up the environment. Instead the taxpayers' money was thrown away on armaments (most of which were never needed). This is a huge loss, that can never be made up, because it represented the savings of the taxpayers for all of those years. It is better though to start late on the task than not at all. At the very least, even if congressional action on the problems cannot be obtained, the President should direct the Army Corps of Engineers to enter an all out effort to clean up our major waterways. I doubt that any partisan political snipers would try to block this—because it is generally understood throughout the land how desperately it is needed. Ecology, of course, is a worldwide problem, and an international effort will be required—

because the very survival of the human race will ultimately be at stake.

Reduction in the use of chemicals, promotion of plant life, and greater restriction of the timber and building industries would be important steps, and a limited restriction upon construction of new roadways might be considered. Also, tighter regulation of the fishing industry might be prudent, as well as more regulation of the hunters who despoil our environment. Wider use of the government's endangered species list would help. With regard to the hunters who now track their diminishing prey with aircraft and telescopic sights—one might wonder (in at least a fanciful way) whether it might not be clever for an international society to be formed, a private group of real sportsmen (killers?), whose game it would be to track the hunters, viz. Richard Connell's famous story "The Most Dangerous Game."

Some degree of environmental pollution is of course inevitable—however amounts of pollutants can be reduced, and some types eliminated. Several suggestions that I want to make in regard to the problem are:

A. The study of the feasibility of the use of wind turbines mounted on tall buildings and on mountainsides—to produce auxiliary power, with very little pollution.

B. More and better insulation used in the structures of all buildings, and more use of double glass or windowless walls—so that less temperature change will occur inside, and less heat and cooling will be required.

C. Another factor that might help reduce air pollution would be for motor vehicles to be built lighter in weight. In this way less fuel would be required to propel them.

D. Perhaps highly radioactive and other extremely toxic wastes could be sealed in containers and stored in certain craters on the moon. This does not have an aesthetic sound, but it is preferable to completely poisoning the earth.

In closing this section I want to discuss in more detail a subject that I merely touched upon in The New Revolution. It is the new field of science known as Cryogenics, science of extreme cold. There are many potential applications for these techniques in such fields as industry and medicine—however the endeavor known as the "freezer program" for the storing of dead bodies, with future reanimation as a goal—this I think to be highly impractical and limited. For those not fully acquainted with it, their idea is that at a future date science will be able to cure the diseases that brought death to these people—thus if the bodies can then be resuscitated it will provide a sort of corporeal immortality. At first glance the idea may sound rather good, but let us examine it further.

First off, people's assets and estates would be tied up permanently, for the purposes of preparing and maintaining their bodies and supposedly for their own use in the future. The long established laws of inheritance would be completely overturned. Thus, upcoming generations of the world would be perpetually cheated in their needs to advance, in preference to human beings who had already lived. All levels of education would be harmed, and higher education might be virtually stopped. The freezer program would be economically unproductive, and an intolerably high financial burden for civilization to bear. And all of this runs contrary to the laws and very intent of nature, the overall plan that the new should continually replace the old!

Secondly, the time factor would be completely scrambled. One might be revived and be alone in the world, his family and friends gone. Or, depending on the length of time, one might be revived and be many years younger than his wife or husband—or much younger than his own children or grandchildren. And these probabilities are not exceptions, mind you—they are the usual way it would be!

Third, the sad condition the world is in, and the inadequacies and failures of human civilization. Few people are interested in the freezer program today, and I doubt that many will be in the future. The promoters of Cryogenics predict that life will be better in the future, in fact they dote upon man's supposed future capabilities. Unfortunately their argument is weak—because throughout human history the discrepancy between what man was capable of and what he actually did has been monumental. We could have had a better world centuries ago, but human beings as a whole will not work toward this end. Instead they spend their resources on war and preparation for war, and their efforts at taking advantage of one another. At the rate the world is going, instead of the future bonanza that the proponents of freezing speak of—a few centuries hence the earth will be so bereft of resources and so polluted that what is left of humanity may have to live underground.

Industry in particular would not be interested in keeping all of its worn out machines, storing them, with the object of rebuilding them in the future. This would run contrary to the entire industrial process, and would certainly impede progress. So it is too with keeping the bodies of those who have already lived (usually worn out and damaged bodies) —it is contrary to the entire scheme of things.

The promoters of freezing speak of future medical science working us over, rebuilding us surgically and biologically. Even if they would or could do this, I hate to think what would finally emerge—and the various techniques that wouldn't quite succeed. Human engineering is for the living, not the dead. Even if we could make it back, we would be strangers in an alien world—terrified at the changes, and as out of place as a ninety year old at a 'teen age dance. We would be no more than curios, and even our own descendants would not want us.

I would like to believe that the freezer program is worthwhile, but I cannot. The Cryogenic techniques, yes—they are valuable to science—but not this program. I would liken it to inmates of a prison, fearing the world outside, and trying to prolong their stay. The attempt is noble, but alas futile.

Remember, the most shameful document on this earth is the history of the human race. It is impossible even to describe the horrendous cruelties and atrocities that dominate it, right up to and including the present. By contrast, it makes even the most rapacious of the other earth creatures appear almost saintly. This world of war, tyrannies, revolutions, murder, disease, corruption, poverty, pain, loneliness, accidents, disasters—This is the world that the proponents of freezing want us to come back to. They hope for betterment, and that is nice—but these feeble hopes, I am afraid, are not good enough. I do not want to come back.

Other far out scientific ideas that will be heard from in the future are: Chemically transferring memory or identity from one person to another, keeping the head or brain alive after bodily death, keeping just the memory alive, disintegration of a body, storing in a computer, then reintegration later, etc., etc. These are macabre things, however, and although in keeping with the wide horizons of scientific research—should nonetheless be carefully watched, administered and supervised by a duly authorized department of government—so that they cannot be misused, get out of hand, or become a menace.

If we waited until our knowledge was complete or fully perfected before we spoke or taught or wrote—there would be no speaking, teaching, or writing. A little fiction, maybe, but certainly no serious work. In short, we learn as we go, just as in all of the professions.

My basic world outlook has changed little over the years —though certain problems have become better clarified.

I do not recommend the course that I followed. It was unnatural, just as any rigorous scientific experiment is unnatural. I proved that it could be done. But beyond this and my various attendant discoveries, the path that I pursued is not one to be emulated. It was difficult as well as precarious. Education—yes, and self-improvement throughout life. But extreme choices are seldom necessary.

Each day that goes by we grow older and the world about us grows older. Yet there can be a great deal of beauty in age. This applies to living as well as inanimate objects. The highly esteemed verdigris on copper and bronze comes with time. The indescribable beauty of autumn leaves comes with age. A new flag or great coat—what are they? But after they have been through battles, then aren't they something! Human beings too can improve and grow more beautiful with age. It is mainly the deeds that they have done—and then their very infirmities become reminders, battle scars, testimony of their past glories.

It is important though that age understand—it should never block or stand in the way of youth. To be truly beautiful, age should retire at the proper time, sit back—and become the diplomat, the financier, the philosopher, the strategist, the adviser—but leave the current battles of life to youth, to carry forward and command. This is the way it should be. But whenever age refuses to step aside and allow youth to assume its rightful position—then age becomes a thing of ugliness, twisted, gnarled, and reminiscent of "The Picture of Dorian Gray." This spectre is seen in numerous fields, but nowhere else is it more evident than in the House of Representatives of the United States Congress, and in the executive branch of some foreign governments.

With regard to men, whenever they seek to cover up their age, they usually succeed only in fooling themselves. The playboy philosophy, too, is really futile—because it is intellectually shallow, and encourages old men to shower money upon young girls, and in general to make fools of themselves. Many women, too, make the mistake of chasing the mirage of youth. One of woman's greatest beauties is actually the depth of understanding come of time and experience. Some women wear their brushed grey better than younger women wear gold and black. It is like the exquisite silver in autumn leaves.

Simple joys are the best in life. Complexity and sophistication of course have their place—but in general the simpler enjoyments are better. The sight of a child's face lighting up upon receiving a treat, is a joy that cannot be measured. The incomparable beauty of the great outdoors—the rapture one can feel from this is above monetary values. Good companionship and being with those we love and respect are more important than high honors. Helping others who need help is more important than fame. And if one has a love in his life that is mutual, then he is unbelievably wealthy.

I have been acquainted with several millionaires. I have also known a great many middle class people, and many of the very poor. Fundamentally one group is hardly better off than the next. The basic joys, strange to relate, show few favorites, and are known to descend just as readily upon a poor household as upon a rich one. The same is true of tragedy. Some wealthy people are unhappy, because, while money can bring advantages and make life more comfortable, it cannot buy happiness. Happiness comes from within, and is a state of mind.

Money is the final product of most human energy. It is a sort of frozen energy—good any time in exchange for goods and services. We need money, especially as we grow older. This is one of the reasons that we save. Most all of us need more money, yet this should never become an object in itself. Remember the simple joys. Some of the wealthiest monarchs throughout history have shown a decided preference for the simpler joys, and have seized upon every opportunity to get away from their exalted positions, however briefly!

And now a few words of advice, especially for younger people:

I stated in The New Revolution, and will now repeat. Be cautious before you enter into matrimony, and insofar as possible, seek out a partner with mental attitudes in common. I always regarded the laws governing divorce as an emergency exit—like a fire escape. It should be there, but is not to be played upon or used frivolously. It is for emergency use only.

Also, be moderate in all of your habits. If you smoke, don't smoke yourself to death. If you drink, don't drink yourself under the table. And regarding drugs, remember— they are for the health, not to play with. Narcotics and hallucinatory agents should not be used, except under the most rigid of professional control.

In finality, we should try to think for ourselves, and help our loved ones. We should aid the unfortunate, and help our country. We should pursue the path of non-violence and vegetarianism. And we should try to develop a sense of fellowship with all of mankind, and a greater respect for other forms of life.

And now, to all of my readers I want to declare that with this critique, I take my leave of you. I have said all that I have to say now, and it is up to the younger generation and the ones beyond that to take up where we left off. I do not intend to do any further writing, although I will remain a philosopher the rest of my life.

In The New Revolution I stated that my opinions were outspokenly honest, and they were. Moreover I had allowed two years to elapse between completion of the original manuscript and publication. Still, the dust had not fully settled. Now it has. There will undoubtedly remain some catalytic effect in The New Revolution. Its major value henceforth however will be in its intellectual depth—and that is what future generations should look to.

To this very day we ask the same age old questions: What is life? What is death? What is truth? What is happiness? And after all of the philosophizing and all of the centuries, and all of the civilizations and all of the misery, and all of the wars and all of the struggle—we still do not know, we still do not have the answers. There are even physical facts about this earth that are as yet unknown, and about the universe we know very little. Our thinking though does point the way toward possible answers.

Some people may wonder, others may think that I belatedly came to religion. The fact is, I had never left—and now have reached a qualified accord. In Chapter V of The New Revolution I stated that I would be willing to end my antagonism toward religion. But first I knew that a vast cleaning of the religious house was needed, before I was ready to settle down. After two world wars in this century and atrocities without number—and the church's main concern still was whether some tavern remained open a little late

80

or some woman sold her affections—I doubt that any sane person would disagree with the premise that a great house-cleaning was needed.

And indeed such a renovation has begun! Americans burning their draft cards, citizens becoming interested in equal rights for all, the churches denouncing war, members of Congress speaking out against the armaments race, war veterans throwing away their medals, sex brought out of the darkness into the open, people becoming concerned about population control and preservation of the environment, etc.

Before I close, I want to state one last thing, that may be of interest to some. I am not really against anyone, as many have supposed, nor do I wish to do battle with anyone, if I can avoid it. In The New Revolution I could not properly state this because of endangering the catalytic effect—however it is so. The only exceptions that I do feel antagonism toward are the politicians who have sold out our country to the armaments industry and military, and the hunters and fishermen who commit crimes against nature. Even these individuals, though, or their descendants might someday be redeemed.

I would respectfully suggest that this guide and companion someday be incorporated into The New Revolution, possibly as a second volume—to be re-published for the human race of the future.

BIBLIOGRAPHY

The following are works that played a part in the development of my mind and philosophy, and I recommend them to others. Most came before The New Revolution, but could not be included. Others came after.

I have excluded from my bibliography no less than 900 books and novels—plus many more journals and periodicals which, although informative and otherwise valuable, were not of sufficient pertinence or reliability to justify inclusion.

I did not follow the usual bibliographical structure, only because this order serves my purpose best. You might note that I included some classical tales of the supernatural, because often they are based upon fact and more voluminously detailed than true accounts.

Afterward—Edith Wharton
Aku-Aku—Thor Heyerdahl, 1958
American Militarism—1970, Viking Press
Auschwitz—Dr. Miklos Nyiszli
Beckoning Fair One, The—Oliver Onions
Bethmoora—Lord Dunsany
Book of the Damned—Chas. Fort
Borderline Oddities—Shelly Lowenkoph
Clausewitz—writings of
Day They Shook The Plum Tree, The—Arthur H. Lewis
Dr. Grimshaw's Sanitarium—Fletcher Pratt
Economy of Death, The—R. J. Barnet
Escape—Ethel Vance, psdm.
Father Flanagan of Boys Town—Oursler, Doubleday
Five Chimneys—Olga Lengyll
Fly, The—George Langelaan
Fools of Time, The—Wm. Edmund Barrett
German Existentialism—Heidegger,
        trans. Dr. Dagobert D. Runes

Ghost Ships of the Great Lakes—Dwight Boyer
Great Boom and Panic, The—Robert T. Patterson
Hedda Gabler—Ibsen
Heine, Heinrich—writings of
Hidden Persuaders, The—Vance Packard
Hitler's Secret Conversations—H. R. Trevor-Roper
Immortality, Scientific Evidence—Alson Smith
Kennedy, Robert F.—Words of
King, Martin Luther—words of
Invisible Horizons—Vincent Gaddis
Life After Death—Hans Holzer
Lincoln—Speeches of
Most Dangerous Game, The—Richard Connell
Municipal Bonds—A. M. Hillhouse, Prentice-Hall
Naked and the Dead, The—Norman Mailer
New York Times, The—compiled, 1963
Nietzsche—Crane Brinton, Harvard Univ. Press, 1941
Of Mice and Men—Steinbeck
Passion in the Desert, A—Balzac
Pentagon Capitalism—Seymour Melman, McGraw-Hill, 1970
Portable Nietzsche, The—Walter Kaufmann
Prominent American Ghosts—Susy Smith, 1967, Dell
Pyramid Climbers, The—Vance Packard
Raintree County—Ross Lockridge, Jr.
Rich and the Super-Rich, The—Ferdinand Lundberg
Right to Bear Arms, The—Carl Bakal
Robinson, E. A.—poems of
Rosenberg, Alfred, Memoirs of
Schweitzer, Albert—Genius in the Jungle, Jos. Gollomb,
    Vanguard
Schweitzer, Albert—The Life and Thought of, Werner Picht,
    Harper & Row
Silent Spring—Rachel Carson
Tamerlane The Earth Shaker—Harold Lamb

They Found My Grave—Joseph Shearing
Time Has Come, The—John Rock, M.D.
True Believer, The—Eric Hoffer
Wait, The—Kit Reed
Wall Street Journal, The—compiled, 1969
Wanderer—Sterling Hayden
Where Their Fire is Not Quenched—May Sinclair
Whitehead, Alfred—writings of
World's Strangest Mysteries, The—Rupert Furneaux
Unearthly, The—Ed. by Kurt Singer

Films, Plays, Music, Art

Action in the North Atlantic
Cleopatra, 1964
Dr. Strangelove
Dr. Zhivago
Elmer Gantry
Enemy Below, The
Escape
Flamingo Road
Head, The
High Noon
House of Wax—Vincent Price
Hucksters, The
Longest Day, The
Razor's Edge, The
Sea Wolf, The
Seven Days in May
8½
***Subject was Roses, The
 **Blowin' in the Wind
 **You'll Never Walk Alone
  *American Gothic—Grant Wood

Like the legendary Phoenix re-born in splendor, The New Revolution lives again— illuminated by a new book from the same author.

This volume goes far toward explaining and exploring many of the intriguing and enigmatical factors of the former work— and should serve as an invaluable aid in its evaluation.

PHILOSOPHY FOR THE NEW AGE also updates several ancient trends of thought, and establishes a new outlook and philosophy for today.